D1337967

T-Pain

by C.F. Earl

Superstars of Hip-Hop

T-Pain

by C.F. Earl

Mason Crest

T-Pain

Mason Crest
370 Reed Road
Broomall, Pennsylvania 19008
www.masoncrest.com

Printed and bound in the United States of America.

First printing
9 8 7 6 5 4 3 2 1

Library of Congress Cataloging-in-Publication Data

Earl, C. F.
  Superstars of hip hop : T-Pain / by C.F. Earl.
    p. cm.
  Includes index.
  ISBN 978-1-4222-2529-5 (hard cover) – ISBN 978-1-4222-2508-0 (series hardcover) – ISBN 978-1-4222-9231-0 (ebook)
  1. T-Pain, 1984--Juvenile literature. 2. Rap musicians–United States–Biography–Juvenile literature. I. Title.
  ML3930.T16E27 2012
  782.421649092–dc23
  [B]
                                    2011020115

Produced by Harding House Publishing Services, Inc.
www.hardinghousepages.com
Interior Design by MK Bassett-Harvey.
Cover design by Torque Advertising & Design.

Publisher's notes:
• All quotations in this book come from original sources and contain the spelling and grammatical inconsistencies of the original text.
• The Web sites mentioned in this book were active at the time of publication. The publisher is not responsible for Web sites that have changed their addresses or discontinued operation since the date of publication. The publisher will review and update the Web site addresses each time the book is reprinted.

DISCLAIMER: The following story has been thoroughly researched, and to the best of our knowledge, represents a true story. While every possible effort has been made to ensure accuracy, the publisher will not assume liability for damages caused by inaccuracies in the data, and makes no warranty on the accuracy of the information contained herein. This story has not been authorized nor endorsed by T-Pain.

Contents

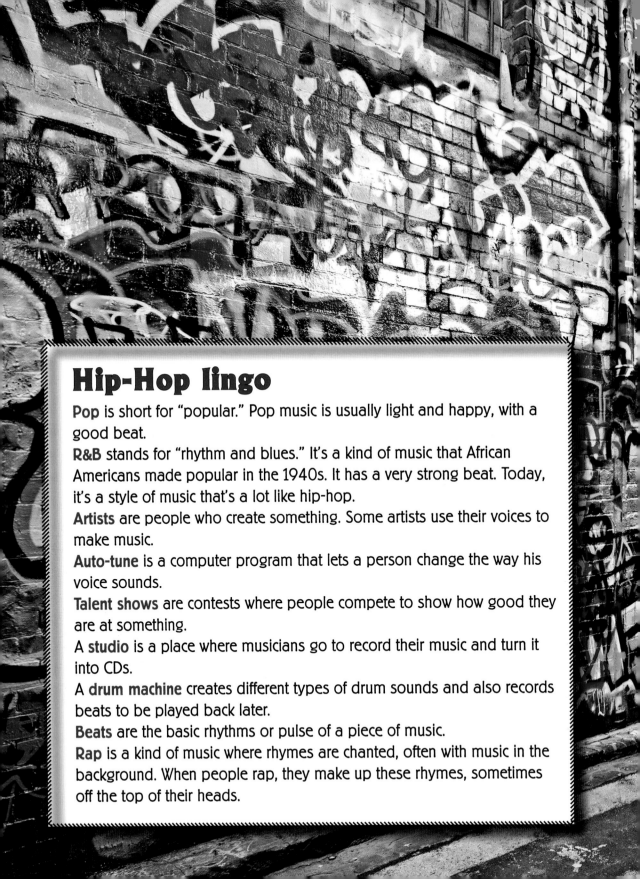

Hip-Hop lingo

Pop is short for "popular." Pop music is usually light and happy, with a good beat.

R&B stands for "rhythm and blues." It's a kind of music that African Americans made popular in the 1940s. It has a very strong beat. Today, it's a style of music that's a lot like hip-hop.

Artists are people who create something. Some artists use their voices to make music.

Auto-tune is a computer program that lets a person change the way his voice sounds.

Talent shows are contests where people compete to show how good they are at something.

A **studio** is a place where musicians go to record their music and turn it into CDs.

A **drum machine** creates different types of drum sounds and also records beats to be played back later.

Beats are the basic rhythms or pulse of a piece of music.

Rap is a kind of music where rhymes are chanted, often with music in the background. When people rap, they make up these rhymes, sometimes off the top of their heads.

Chapter 1

T-Pain's Beginnings

Today, T-Pain is one of music's biggest stars. His music is known around the world. His songs can be heard on the radio, on TV, and in clubs. You can hear his voice on songs by some of the biggest names in hip-hop, **pop**, and **R&B**.

Many **artists** have used T-Pain's style since he started making music. Rappers like Kanye West and Lil Wayne have used his **auto-tune** style. Singers like Usher, Justin Bieber, and Mariah Carey have also used auto-tune since T-Pain made it famous.

T-Pain may be a star today, but he didn't always have it so good. He was once just a boy making music in his bedroom. T-Pain was once a kid from Florida trying to reach his dreams.

Early Life

T-Pain's real name is Faheem Rasheed Najm. He was born on September 30, 1985, in Tallahassee, Florida. Faheem's father was Shasheem Najm. His mother was Aliyah Najm. They were both Muslim.

Both Aliyah and Shasheem loved music. Shasheem had done some rapping. Aliyah had sung in some **talent shows** before meeting Shasheem. Like his parents, young Faheem always loved music. And Aliyah and Shasheem always supported that love.

Growing up in Tallahassee was hard for Faheem. Lots of people in Tallahassee were poor. Bullies also gave Faheem a hard time at school. Because Faheem was Muslim, he had to deal with being different from many other Tallahassee kids.

T-Pain at Ten

When Faheem was just 10 years old, he started making music. Shasheem found a keyboard by the side of the road and brought it home. He gave it to Faheem.

Faheem loved music. But he didn't know how to play. He listened to songs on the radio. Then he tried to learn to play them on the keyboard. Soon, Faheem had taught himself to play some piano.

It wasn't long before Faheem turned his bedroom into a recording **studio**. He used his keyboard and a **drum machine**. Faheem started writing and recording songs right away. He made **beats** and rapped over them. He also started singing his own songs.

Faheem loved **rap** and R&B. He wanted to make both kinds of music. He wanted to be a singer and a rapper. Some musicians might only do one or the other—but Faheem wanted to make as many different kinds of music as he could.

Music was a way for Faheem to stay away from the bullies that bothered him. He could get out what he was feeling by rapping or singing. He was still young, but Faheem had big dreams. He wanted to make it out of Tallahassee. He wanted to become a star in music. Faheem knew he had talent. All it would take was some hard work.

T-Pain Joins Nappy Headz

Faheem kept making music in his room. He worked hard to get better and better at making songs. Faheem rapped and sang more and more. It wasn't long before Faheem got a chance to make music with a Tallahassee rap group. Faheem was a teenager when he joined Nappy Headz. Soon, Faheem started using the name T-Pain.

Nappy Headz started recording music together. The group got some of their songs played on the radio in Tallahassee. Soon, the group was beginning to get fans in Florida and other southeastern states. Their songs "Robbery" and "F.L.A." became small hits.

Nappy Headz was a way for T-Pain to work on music. It gave him a taste of his dream of becoming a hip-hop artist. He wanted so badly to make it in music. He'd been working on his dream since he was just ten. Now, he had a chance to make his dreams come true.

Tallahassee Pain

T-Pain stands for "Tallahassee Pain." For T-Pain, the name is about all the pain he went through growing up in Tallahassee. He had to deal with bullies. He had to deal with growing up in an area that didn't have a lot of money. He had to deal with growing up in the country, when all his dreams seemed to be in big cities.

Most of all, though, "T-Pain" is about the pain of working hard to make it in music. T-Pain had to struggle to get his music heard. Growing up in Tallahassee, he was far from his musical dreams. He told an interviewer that it was hard to reach his goals in music from Tallahassee.

T-Pain may be a star today, but he grew up in a rural area of Florida that seemed far away from the music business. T-Pain would have to work hard to break into making music.

"If you are trying to get into the music industry, it's hard to get somebody to come to Tallahassee and listen," he said. "It's the same pain in any country life."

T-Pain had started to chase his dreams of making music. He'd gone from making songs in his bedroom to rapping with Nappy Headz. He wasn't as famous as he would become later, but T-Pain wasn't far from getting the break he needed. And soon, the world would know his name.

Hip-Hop lingo

An **album** is a group of songs collected together on a CD.
A **record label** is a company that produces music for singers and groups and puts out CDs.
Singles are songs that are sold by themselves.
The **singles chart** is a list of the best-selling songs for a week.
A **remix** is a new version of a song that has already been put out.
Ringtones are pieces of songs that play when a call comes in to a cell phone.
Digital downloads are copies of a song or album that are bought on the Internet and copied directly to a computer, instead of being bought in a store as a CD.

Chapter 2

T-Pain Finds His Voice

T-Pain had started his life in music. He and Nappy Headz had done pretty well. But soon, the group split up. The members of the group went off to make their own music. T-Pain did the same. He started recording new songs without the group.

T-Pain Turns Singer

Without Nappy Headz, T-Pain could do what he wanted. He knew he could do more than rap. As a kid, he'd sung songs in his bedroom. Now, T-Pain started singing more in his music. It wasn't long before he was singing more than he was rapping. T-Pain was recording his own songs again, just like he had in his bedroom as a kid.

Soon, T-Pain recorded a whole **album**'s worth of songs. He put out the album himself. He started his own **record label**. The label was called Hard n' B. Hard n' B was T-Pain's name for his kind of music. It was R&B mixed with rap's toughness.

One song on T-Pain's self-made album was even played on the radio in Tallahassee. T-Pain may not have been famous yet, but he was making the music he wanted to make.

He's told interviewers that he didn't want to be just another R&B artist or rapper. "Everybody was doing the same thing," he said. "Everybody wanted to rap. . . . But I came with something different. You can't help but notice."

T-Pain's different style helped him stand out. His Hard n' B sound was starting to catch on.

T-Pain's big break came when he recorded a version of Akon's song "Locked Up" in 2005. People liked T-Pain's version of the song. It became a small hit. T-Pain even made a video for it. T-Pain's version of the song soon made its way to Akon himself.

Akon heard the song and listened to some of T-Pain's other music. He loved T-Pain's take on R&B music. He thought T-Pain's sound could be the next big thing in music. He found a way to get in touch with the young Tallahassee singer. When Akon phoned T-Pain, though, T-Pain just hung up. He couldn't believe that the real Akon would be calling him. After all, he was just a young singer from Florida. Akon was a star. But after a few more tries, Akon finally talked to T-Pain.

Akon told T-Pain he wanted to sign him to his record label. Soon, T-Pain was part of Akon's Konvict Music. T-Pain started work on his first album right away.

Rappa Ternt Sanga

The name of T-Pain's first album said it all. He called the album *Rappa Ternt Sanga* (Rapper Turned Singer). The album came out on December 6, 2005.

T-Pain started working on *Rappa Ternt Sanga* in the fall of 2005. He wrote and produced many of the songs on the album. Most new artists don't always get that chance. T-Pain had been making music since he was 10, though. He knew what he was doing. But he didn't do it all by himself. He got to work with some great rap artists on *Rappa Ternt Sanga*. Mike Jones, Bone Crusher, Styles P, and Tay Dizm all worked on songs for the album. Akon also worked with T-Pain on two songs for *Rappa Ternt Sanga*.

T-Pain put out three **singles** from *Rappa Ternt Sanga*. The first single was called "I'm Sprung." T-Pain wrote the song for his wife, Amber. The two have been married since 2003. "I'm Sprung" came out on August 16, 2005, before the album came out.

T-Pain's first album, *Rappa Ternt Sanga*, had more than one hit single and helped make T-Pain the star he is today.

"I'm Sprung" was a huge hit for T-Pain. The song reached number eight on the *Billboard* **singles chart**. It also made it to number nine on the R&B singles chart and number 17 on the pop singles chart. "I'm Sprung" was T-Pain's first top-ten hit, but it wouldn't be his last.

"I'm Sprung" wasn't just a hit in the United States. It was popular around the world. The song made it onto the charts in Ireland, Australia, the UK, and Finland. "I'm Sprung" was such a hit in the UK that T-Pain recorded a UK **remix** of the song. The UK remix features UK rap star Dizzee Rascal. In the United States, another remix of "I'm Sprung" featured rappers Trick Daddy and YoungBloodZ.

"I'm Sprung" sold very well. The song didn't just sell by itself, either. In the United States alone, "I'm Sprung" has sold more than a million **ringtones** for cell phones.

The second single from the album was called "I'm N Luv." T-Pain put out the single on December 13, 2005. The song was an even bigger hit than the first single from *Rappa Ternt Sanga*. "I'm N Luv" reached number five on the singles chart. On the R&B singles chart, the song reached number ten. The song was even a hit on the pop singles chart, where it reached number seven. In the UK, the song made it to number 38 on the singles chart.

The second single from *Rappa Ternt Sanga* sold even better than the first. It sold three million ringtones. It also sold more than half a million **digital downloads**.

The album's third single was called "Studio Luv." The song came out on October 2, 2006. It didn't do as well as the first two singles. The song didn't make it onto the charts. Later, T-Pain recorded a remix of the song featuring Lil Wayne.

Rappa Ternt Sanga was a huge hit. In its first week out, the album sold more than 45,000 copies. In the same week, *Rappa Ternt*

Akon gave T-Pain the chance to make it in the music world after hearing the Florida singer's take on one of his own songs.

T-Pain's sound inspired artists from Kanye West to Lil Wayne. Wayne's song "Lollipop" features the rapper singing using auto-tune.

Sanga made it to number 40 on the *Billboard* album chart. Soon, it reached number 33. By the end of 2010, the album had sold more than 800,000 copies.

T-Pain and Auto-Tune

Before he had a record deal with Akon, T-Pain had been using auto-tune on many songs. Auto-tune is a computer program that can change the sound of a singer's voice. With auto-tune, a singer can hit more notes than he might be able to without it. It can make a singer sound a bit like a robot. It can also be used to help a singer hit many notes more quickly than they usually could.

Not everyone is a fan of auto-tune. Some people say that singers shouldn't use it. They say that auto-tune helps people who can't really sing sound like they can. T-Pain knows he really can sing, though. After *Rappa Ternt Sanga* came out, he sang without auto-tune at his shows. He wanted to prove to his fans that he could sing without it.

T-Pain uses auto-tune to get a sound that's different from other artists. He knew he had to do something to stand out in a music world that has so many artists. So he started using auto-tune on some of his songs. He doesn't use it on every song, but auto-tune has helped T-Pain stand out. It's also come to be what many people know T-Pain for.

T-Pain was living his dreams. He'd gone from rapping with Nappy Headz to being one of hip-hop's newest stars. His first album, *Rappa Ternt Sanga*, had been a hit. He'd also started working with some of the biggest artists in hip-hop. Thanks to Akon and a little bit of luck, T-Pain was on his way to taking over the music world.

Hip-Hop lingo

Each year, the National Academy of Recording Arts and Sciences gives out the **Grammy Awards** (short for Gramophone Awards)—or Grammys—to people who have done something really big in the music industry. When someone has been **nominated**, he has been picked as one of the people who might win an award.

A **collaboration** is when two or more people work together on a project.

Chapter 3

T-Pain's Epiphany

After joining Akon's Konvict Music label, T-Pain got his shot at fame. And he took it! His album *Rappa Ternt Sanga* was a huge hit for a new artist. Soon, T-Pain was hard at work on a new company. He was also working on a new album.

Nappy Boy Entertainment

In 2006, T-Pain started his own record label. He called the new company Nappy Boy Entertainment. T-Pain worked with Jive Records to get Nappy Boy's music out. Jive also worked with Akon's Konvict Music.

T-Pain worked hard to sign artists to his new label. He signed on singer Shawnna. She had been with Ludacris's Disturbing Tha Peace Records. T-Pain also signed rappers Tay Dizm and Young Cash. Singing groups Sophia Fresh and One Chance also joined Nappy Boy.

Later, T-Pain would sign rapper Travie McCoy to the label. He'd been with a band called Gym Class Heroes. His first solo album would come out with help from Nappy Boy in 2010.

T-Pain put out his second album on Nappy Boy. It was the first album that Nappy Boy released. Now, T-Pain was making music and running his own business.

Epiphany

T-Pain's second album was called *Epiphany*. T-Pain put out *Epiphany* on June 5, 2007.

An epiphany is a sudden realization. If you have an epiphany, you might realize something you didn't understand before. T-Pain told his fans that his own epiphany was that he needed to be himself. He realized that he didn't need to follow other people's paths to success. He just needed to be himself and record the music he wanted. T-Pain saw that he had his own style. He saw that his fans wanted him to keep doing things his way.

T-Pain worked on *Epiphany* after *Rappa Ternt Sanga* became a hit. Just as he did with *Rappa Ternt Sanga*, T-Pain wrote and produced most of the songs on *Epiphany*. He also got to work with many big names in hip-hop. T-Pain recorded songs for *Epiphany* with singers Akon and Shawnna. He also recorded with rappers Yung Joc, Kardinal Offishall, and Tay Dizm.

The first single from *Epiphany* was called "Buy U a Drank." The song featured Yung Joc. The single came out on February 20, 2007. The song was a giant hit for T-Pain. It made it to number one on the singles chart. It also reached the top spot on the R&B singles chart. On the pop singles chart, the song reached number four. It was T-Pain's third top-ten hit in just two years.

"Buy U a Drank" was a hit around the world, too. The song made it onto the singles charts in Australia, Canada, and the UK. In New Zealand and the UK, the song made it to the number-two position.

Rolling Stone magazine named "Buy U a Drank" number 63 on their list of the hundred best songs of 2007. In just a few months,

Thanks to hit songs like "Buy U a Drank" and "Bartender," *Epiphany* was a huge hit for T-Pain.

the song had sold millions of ringtones and more than a million downloads.

The second single from the album was called "Bartender." The song featured T-Pain's friend Akon. The single came out on June 7, 2007. Like "Buy U a Drank," the song was a big hit.

"Bartender" reached number five on the singles chart in the United States. On the R&B singles chart, the song made it to num-

Rapper Flo Rida and T-Pain had a massive hit with "Low." The song helped both artists to become more famous and popular with fans.

ber nine. It also reached number 10 on the pop singles chart. The song was a hit in New Zealand and Canada, too. It hit number one on the New Zealand singles chart.

The third single from *Epiphany* was called "Church." The song came out on October 2, 2007. The song was a hit in the UK, New Zealand, and Canada. It made it onto singles charts in each of those countries.

Epiphany was a huge hit. When the album came out, it went to number one on the albums chart. In its first week out, the album sold more than 170,000 copies. Less than a year after it came out, it had sold around 819,000 copies. T-Pain had another hit album. *Epiphany*'s singles did even better than those on *Rappa Ternt Sanga*. And while T-Pain's own music was very popular, he was also making hits with other artists.

The Man with the Golden Touch

In 2007, T-Pain was working with many of music's biggest artists. He teamed up with Flo Rida for one of the biggest hits of the year. The song was called "Low." It was one of the highest selling singles of 2007. It stayed at number one on the singles chart longer than any other song that year.

T-Pain also recorded a song called "Good Life" with Kanye West. "Good Life" was a huge hit for Kanye and T-Pain. It reached number seven on the singles chart.

T-Pain worked with other artists, too. He worked with singer Chris Brown on "Kiss Kiss." The song went to number one on the singles chart. He also worked with R&B great R. Kelly. The two recorded a remix of R. Kelly's "I'm a Flirt" with rapper T.I.

T-Pain was riding high in the music world. After *Rappa Ternt Sanga*, everyone wanted to work with him. His auto-tune style was

T-Pain and Kanye West worked together on the Grammy-winning song "Good Life" from Kanye's album *Graduation*.

becoming more and more popular all the time. The young man from Tallahassee was getting to work with music's biggest stars.

The 2008 **Grammy Awards** were held on February 10, 2008. T-Pain was up for four awards that night. He and Akon had been **nominated** for Best R&B Performance by a Duo or Group for "Bartender." T-Pain and singer Chris Brown were up for Best Rap/Sung **Collaboration** for "Kiss Kiss." T-Pain and Kanye West's "Good Life" was up for Best Rap/Sung Collaboration and Best Rap Song.

T-Pain and Kanye ended up winning Best Rap Song with "Good Life." It was the first Grammy he had ever won. But it wouldn't be T-Pain's last.

Hip-Hop lingo

A **digital record label** is a company that sells its music online.

Chapter 4

T-Pain's Circus

T-Pain was riding high after he won his first Grammy. Both his first and second albums had been big hits. He'd had hit singles. He'd worked with other artists to make hit songs. T-Pain's sound was also starting to take on a life of its own.

After T-Pain started to use auto-tune, other artists began to use it too. In 2008, rappers Kanye West and Lil Wayne both used auto-tune. Kanye put out an album called *808s & Heartbreak*. On the album, Kanye uses auto-tune on almost every song. Lil Wayne used auto-tune on his own hit song "Lollipop."

T-Pain had made it in music. He'd gotten so big that other artists had even started to use his style and sound. People just couldn't get enough of T-Pain and his auto-tuned singing.

T-Pain Takes Nappy Boy Digital

In 2008, T-Pain told interviewers and fans that he had a new idea for his record company. He wanted to make Nappy Boy Entertainment into a **digital record label**.

After the release of *Thr33 Ringz*, T-Pain changed his stage show into something much closer to a circus than a hip-hop concert.

T-Pain told fans that he was going to put out most of Nappy Boy's music over the Internet. The label would put out music through iTunes and ringtones. T-Pain said the label would still release some music in stores on CD. But most of Nappy Boy's music would only come out online.

T-Pain had lots of success selling his music online. He sold millions of his songs as ringtones for cell phones. Many of his singles have also sold very well as digital downloads. In today's music world, an artist can sell millions without having a CD in stores. More and more people are using the Internet to get their music. To keep up, artists like T-Pain have to think of new ways of doing business.

Thr33 Ringz

T-Pain called his third album *Thr33 Ringz*. He told interviewers that the name of the album came from a friend. T-Pain said the friend told him he was in charge of the circus of the hip-hop music world. T-Pain liked the idea. He worked it into the name of his new album. *Thr33 Ringz* came out on November 11, 2008.

T-Pain wrote and produced all the songs on *Thr33 Ringz*. He also created a character called "Ringleader Man" for the album. He made three skits for the album that show off the character. A song called "Ringleader Man" introduced the character.

T-Pain put out three singles from *Thr33 Ringz*. The first was called "Can't Believe It." The song featured T-Pain's friend Lil Wayne. The single came out on July 29, 2008. T-Pain also recorded a remix of the song with Justin Timberlake. The remix came out on November 7, 2008.

"Can't Believe It" was a big hit. In the United States, the song reached number seven on the singles chart. It made it to number two on the R&B singles chart. "Can't Believe It" was also a small hit in other countries. The song made it onto singles charts in the UK, New Zealand, and Canada.

The second single from *Thr33 Ringz* was called "Chopped & Skrewed." The song featured rapper Ludacris. The song came out on September 23, 2008. It was hit, but not as big as the first single. It reached number 27 on the singles chart. On the R&B chart, the song reached number three, though.

Thr33 Ringz was another successful album for T-Pain. The album might not have done as well as his others, but it still sold well and made fans happy.

The third single from the album was "Freeze." "Freeze" featured singer Chris Brown. It came out in October 2008. "Freeze" didn't do as well as the first two singles on *Thr33 Ringz*, though. The song was a hit, but not as big as some of T-Pain's other songs. It reached number 38 on the singles chart.

Thr33 Ringz was another hit album for T-Pain. In its first week out, it sold more than 165,000 copies. In just a few months, it sold more than 500,000 copies.

At the 2009 Grammy Awards, T-Pain was up for three awards. T-Pain and Flo Rida were nominated for Best Rap Song for "Low." The two were also up for Best Rap/Sung Collaboration. T-Pain had two songs in the category. He and Lil Wayne were also nominated for Best Rap/Sung Collaboration for their song "Got Money."

T-Pain didn't take home any awards that night, but he was still at the top of the music world. The biggest names in music show up at the Grammys. T-Pain was now among them.

Hip-Hop lingo

A **soundtrack** is a collection of all the songs on a movie.
A **mixtape** is a collection of a few songs put on a CD or given away for free on the Internet without being professionally recorded.

Chapter 5

T-Pain Takes Over

By the end of 2009, T-Pain had taken over the music world. He was working with lots of artists. He seemed to be on every hit song. You could hardly turn on the radio without hearing T-Pain or someone who was using his style. The year 2009 had also brought T-Pain several Grammy Award nominations.

The 2010 Grammy Awards were held on January 31, 2010. At the awards show, T-Pain performed "Blame It" with Jamie Foxx. It was T-Pain's first time performing at the Grammys.

T-Pain was nominated for four Grammys that night. He was up for Best Rap/Sung Collaboration for "I'm on a Boat" with The Lonely Island. He and Jamie Foxx were nominated for Best R&B Song and Best R&B Performance by a Duo or Group for "Blame It." T-Pain's album *Thr33 Ringz* was also up for Best Contemporary Album.

T-Pain and Jamie Foxx ended up winning Best R&B Performance by a Duo or a Group for "Blame It." T-Pain had won another Grammy. He'd been up against some of the greatest artists in hip-hop, pop, and

R&B. T-Pain's name was right next to the names of the biggest stars in music.

T-Pain Branches Out

T-Pain's dream had always been to make music. But by 2010, he was also trying new things. He was moving into doing some acting, working in TV and movies.

In 2010, T-Pain even put out his own cartoon for Cartoon Network's Adult Swim. He called the cartoon movie *Freaknik: The Musical.*

Freaknik starred some of the biggest names in rap and R&B. Rappers like Lil Wayne, Snoop Dogg, Rick Ross, Mack Maine, and Big Boi all worked on *Freaknik.* Actors Charlie Murphy, Andy Samberg, and Kel Mitchell lent their voices to the movie. R&B singer Kelis played both Tyra Banks and Oprah Winfrey in *Freaknik.* T-Pain got some of music's biggest stars—and his good friends—to help him make the movie.

Freaknik was a hit with Adult Swim fans. When it aired on March 7, 2010, almost 800,000 people watched.

T-Pain also worked on a **soundtrack** album for *Freaknik.* The soundtrack came out on April 20, 2010. The album had five songs on it. All the songs were recorded by T-Pain as the Ghost of Freaknik, his character from the movie. The songs on the soundtrack also featured some of the rappers from the movie. Snoop Dogg, Rick Ross, Mack Maine, and Young Cash helped out on songs for the soundtrack.

In 2010, T-Pain also worked on some acting. He was in a movie called *Lottery Ticket.* He played a character named Junior. The movie starred rappers Bow Wow and Ice Cube. It also starred actors Bill Bellamy, Keith David, and Mike Epps. *Lottery Ticket* was T-Pain's first movie role, but he'd done other acting before.

bow brandon t. naturi keith charlie gbenga
WOW JACKSON NAUGHTON DAVID MURPHY AKINNAGBE
terry bill mike loretta ice
CREWS BELLAMY EPPS T-PAIN DEVINE ...CUBE

Lottery ticket

Winning is just the beginning. Surviving is another story.

I DID NOT WIN THE LOTTERY

With *Lottery Ticket*, T-Pain was able to show fans another side of himself. T-Pain can do much more than make great music!

Before he did *Freaknik*, T-Pain had worked on another cartoon. He'd worked on a show called *Aqua Teen Hunger Force*. Like *Freaknik*, the show was on Cartoon Network's Adult Swim. T-Pain was in two episodes. He'd also worked on another Adult Swim show, called *Robot Chicken*. T-Pain had done one episode of that show in 2009.

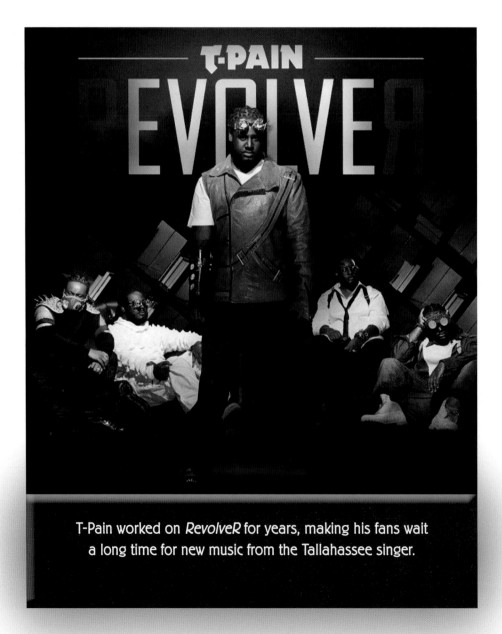

T-Pain worked on *RevolveR* for years, making his fans wait a long time for new music from the Tallahassee singer.

T-Pain also worked in commercials. In 2010, he acted in an ad for Toshiba computers. He was also in a Bud Light commercial. In the Bud Light ad, T-Pain and other actors sang using auto-tune.

RevolveR

T-Pain's fourth album was meant to come out soon after *Thr33 Ringz*. But instead, T-Pain worked on it for years, while he did other things. The album is called *RevolveR*.

T-Pain started putting out new songs in late 2009. He told fans that the new songs were singles from his next album. But when *RevolveR* finally came out in 2011, the new songs weren't on the album. The first new song was called "Take Your Shirt Off." It came out in November 2009.

The next song came out in early 2010. This second single featured Young Jeezy. It wasn't long before T-Pain put out another version of the song. The second version didn't have Young Jeezy's verse on it.

T-Pain said his next single, "Rap Song," was from *RevolveR*. The song featured rapper Rick Ross. "Rap Song" came out in October, 2010. The song didn't do as well as T-Pain would have liked, though.

T-Pain was also working with other artists on their music. He worked on the remix to Wiz Khalifa's hit song "Black and Yellow." He sang on the DJ Khaled song "All I Do Is Win" and Welcome to My Hood."

In March 2011, T-Pain put out "Best Love Song," the first official single from *RevolveR*. The song featured singer Chris Brown. The song reached number 33 on the singles charts in the United States. "Best Love Song" also did well in the UK and Australia.

In May, T-Pain put out a **mixtape** of new songs called *Prevolver.* T-Pain wanted to make sure his fans had new music to listen to while they waited for *RevolveR*.

In September, T-Pain released a new single with singer Lily Allen and rapper Wiz Khalifa. The song was called "5 O'Clock." The song made it into the top ten on the U.S. singles charts. "5 O'Clock" was also a hit in countries around the world.

T-Pain finally released his fourth album, *RevolveR*, in December 2011. Fans had waited for years for T-Pain's next album. T-Pain worked with many different artists on *RevolveR*. The album features Lil Wayne, Chris Brown, Ne-Yo, Pitbull, and others.

In its first week out, *RevolveR* made it to number 28 on the *Billboard* album charts. The album didn't do as well as T-Pain's others, but fans were happy to have *RevolveR* in their hands after so many years of waiting!

Looking to the Future

T-Pain has done more in just a few years than most artists can do in a lifetime. He's recorded hit songs and big albums. He's sold more albums and singles than most artists can dream of. He's worked with some of music's biggest names.

Once just a kid making music in his bedroom in Tallahassee, today T-Pain is a star. His music can be heard on the radio and on TV. Now, you can even see his face in commercials. You can hear his voice on TV shows. T-Pain has worked hard to get where he is. And now he's living his childhood dreams of making it in the music world.

T-Pain has helped to shape the sound of hip-hop, R&B, and pop. His auto-tuned style of singing has been used by some of the biggest artists in the world. Though not everyone is a fan of the style, it has become very popular. Artists making almost every kind of music have used T-Pain's style. Few artists can say they've changed the sound of popular music as much as T-Pain can.

After the release of his fourth album, *RevolveR*, T-Pain is keeping busy. He's performing for audiences around the world. He's working on new music with different artists. He's running Nappy Boy Entertainment. T-Pain has had amazing success with his music, and he wants to make sure that he keeps his success going!

It seems there's nothing that can stop the young man from Tallahassee from doing the things he wants to. And his fans just can't get enough T-Pain. They'll wait patiently for whatever comes next from the singer.

1985 Faheem Rasheed Najm (or "T-Pain") is born on September 30, 1985 in Tallahassee, Florida.

1995 T-Pain turns his bedroom into a music studio. He uses a keyboard, a drum machine, and a four-track recorder.

2004 T-Pain joins the rap group Nappy Headz to make a cover of Akon's song "Locked Up." The cover is a big hit.

2005 T-Pain releases his first album, *Rappa Ternt Sanga*.

Two singles from *Rappa Ternt Sanga* reach the top ten on the charts.

2007 T-Pain's second album, *Epiphany*, comes out. It sells 819,000 records in the United States.

The album's first single, "Buy U a Drank (Shawty Snappin')," reaches number one on the charts.

The album's second single, "Bartender," reaches number five on the charts.

2008 T-Pain teams up with Kanye West to make the song "Good Life." It goes on to win a BET Award and a Grammy Award for Best Rap Song.

T-Pain's third album comes out, called *Thr33 Ringz*. The album has three singles, "Can't Believe It," "Chopped 'N' Skrewed," and "Freeze."

2009 In February, T-Pain appears on *Saturday Night Live*.

In May, T-Pain gives his voice to the show *Aqua Teen Hunger Force*.

In June, students try to elect T-Pain as president of Florida State University.

2010   T-Pain takes part in the "We Are the World 25 for Haiti" single.

        T-Pain's *Freaknik: The Musical* airs on Adult Swim.

        T-Pain appears in *Lottery Ticket.*

2011   T-Pain releases *RevolveR.*

In Books

Baker, Soren. *The History of Rap and Hip Hop*. San Diego, Calif.: Lucent, 2006.

Comissiong, Solomon W. F. *How Jamal Discovered Hip-Hop Culture*. New York: Xlibris, 2008.

Cornish, Melanie. *The History of Hip Hop*. New York: Crabtree, 2009.

Czekaj, Jef. *Hip and Hop, Don't Stop!* New York: Hyperion, 2010.

Haskins, Jim. *One Nation Under a Groove: Rap Music and Its Roots*. New York: Jump at the Sun, 2000.

Hatch, Thomas. *A History of Hip-Hop: The Roots of Rap*. Portsmouth, N.H.: Red Bricklearning, 2005.

Websites

Official T-Pain Site
www.t-pain.net

T-Pain Fan Site
nappyboyonline.com/profile/Tpain

T-Pain on AOL
music.aol.com/artist/t-pain

T-Pain on MTV
www.mtv.com/music/artist/t_pain/artist.jhtml

T-Pain on Myspace
www.myspace.com/tpain

Discography

Albums

2005	Rappa Ternt Sanga
2007	Epiphany
2008	Thr33 Ringz
2011	RevolveR

Index

About the Author

C.F. Earl is a writer living and working in Binghamton, New York. Earl writes mostly on social and historical topics, including health, the military, and finances. An avid student of the world around him, and particularly fascinated with almost any current issue, C.F. Earl hopes to continue to write for books, websites, and other publications for as long as he is able.

Picture Credits